TARJETA POSTAL

POSTCARDS FROM THE BASQUE COUNTRY

A Journey of Enchantment and Imagination

12 Tarjetas Postales Destacables
Cartes Postales Detachables

By Beth Nelson

STEWART, TABORI & CHANG
NEW YORK

Eskerrik Asko--to all the Basque people who made me feel that this was always home, and to the village of Fuenterrabia--Gora Hondarribia!

The author gratefully acknowledges those who have given kind permission to reproduce material contained in this volume. A complete list of credits and permissions can be found on the last page of this book as an extension of this copyright notice.

Published in 1999 by
Stewart, Tabori & Chang
A division of U.S. Media Holdings, Inc.
115 West 18th Street
New York, NY 10011

Distributed in Canada by
General Publishing Company Ltd.
30 Lesmill Road
Don Mills, Ontario, Canada M3B 2T6

Library of Congress Cataloging-in-Publication Data
Nelson, Beth.
Postcards from the Basque Country : a journey of
enchantment and imagination / by Beth Nelson.
   p.   cm.
 ISBN 1-55670-893-9 (alk. paper)
 1. País Vasco (Spain)--Description and travel. 2. Pays Basque
(France)--Description and travel. 3. Nelson, Beth--Journeys--Spain--
País Vaso. 4. Nelson, Beth--Journeys--France--Pays Basque.
 I. Title.
DP302.B46N45   1999   98-55675
914.6'60483--dc21   CIP

Printed in Hong Kong

10 9 8 7 6 5 4 3 2 1

First Printing

"Traveller, there is no path.
Paths are made by walking."

"Caminante, no hay camino
Se hace camino al andar."

(Antonio Machado)

DREAMS

When I was young, my grandmother told me stories.

SUEÑOS

WHEN I WAS YOUNG, MY GRANDMOTHER TOLD ME STORIES. SHE HAD LEARNED THIS FROM HER FATHER, AND HE FROM HIS FATHER BEFORE HIM. ALONG WITH THESE STORIES, SHE ENCOURAGED THE KEEPING OF A JOURNAL.

BOTH WERE FORMS OF CELEBRATING THE ORDINARY; BOTH WERE EVIDENCE OF ONE'S LIVING. SHE HAD A BELIEF THAT <u>IDLENESS BRED DISCONTENT</u>, AND THAT THE DAILY EMPTYING OF ONE'S THOUGHTS ONTO PAPER MADE ROOM FOR NEW IMAGININGS.

SHE TAUGHT ME THESE THINGS AS A WAY OF DREAMING.

MY GRANDMOTHER BECAME A TRAVELLER AT QUITE A LATE AGE, BUT BETWEEN HER SIXTY-FIFTH AND NINETIETH YEAR, SHE MANAGED TO SEE ABOUT HALF THE WORLD. EACH JOURNEY BROUGHT BACK TALES TO TELL. EACH JOURNEY BECAME A RECORD OF HER LIVING.

I, TOO, BECAME A TRAVELLER. I LOOKED FOR THE
FAMILIAR IN THE FOREIGN, AND OFTEN FOUND
ENCHANTMENT IN THE EVERYDAY. THE FARTHER I
WENT, THE CLOSER I FELT TO WHERE I CAME FROM.

THE POWER OF MEMORY SEEMS MADE OF THESE
IMAGININGS. MEMORY, AND A LITTLE STORY OF LOVE
LONG AGO, BROUGHT ME BACK HERE. WE ARE ALL
STORYTELLERS, AND THIS WAS MY FIRST STORY, IN A
PLACE THAT FELT LIKE HOME, WHERE I'D NEVER BEEN
BEFORE.

MY GRANDMOTHER TOLD ME THAT "DISTANCE
IS NOTHING; IT IS ONLY THE FIRST STEP THAT IS
DIFFICULT." AND SO, AT THE START OF ANOTHER
JOURNEY, I DEDICATE THIS BOOK TO HER, WITH LOVE
AND ALL MY AFFECTION.

CÔTE BASQUE

19 JULIO, 1998

S U E Ñ O S . . .

She taught me these things, as a way of dreaming.

"Distance is the great maker of fantasies."

Walking through a Manhattan night I think of Lorca

arriving from Spain, a poet in New York.

I make my way to the Empire State Building, for

one last look,   at the "city that never slee

SOUVENIR OF VISIT TO THE
MOST FAMOUS
BUILDING IN THE WORLD
EMPIRE STATE
OBSERVATORIES
245847

Taking the lift to the top,   I see I am surrounded

by lovers,

and the murmer of sweet nothings in

many languages.

Far below, the cars seem like a distant, dazzling

river of light. Everything reduced to the

seductive scale of skyscraper.

Tonight the sign reads "Unlimited Visibility"

POETA EN NUEVA YORK

and if I look carefully

I can almost see Spain

in the distance.

4

(ON THE AEROPLANE)

VIA AIR MAIL

julio

High above the clouds I'm thinking,

What is it that makes certain places, feel like home

Perhaps that is what this story is all about.

A love affair with a time and place, that has remained

in my mind, like a melody.

They say "Distance is the great maker of fantasies"

and I have a small crisis of confidence, high over the

Atlantic, cases packed with art supplies and memory.

I'm going to the Basque Country to

paint and write, and perhaps find what I've been searching for.

The pilot announces we are passing over France now,

beginning the long descent.

I can see the Bay of Biscay out my window, and I have this

feeling of certainty

I'm coming home.

Basque

"The end of all our exploring

will be to arrive where we started

and know the place, for the first time."

T.S. Eliot

My Dear Tenn,

Finally I am able to write after what feels like a long journey. I have landed in a small fishing village off the Bay of Biscay, five minutes by ferry to France. The boat is as charming as you can imagine. It flies the French tricolor, the Basque, and the Spanish flags with passengers just as colorful. All shapes and sizes, all manner of language floats through the air during the crossing. One can see France across the Txingudi Bay, the only thing separating it from Spain. The little harbour is filled to capacity with every type of fishing and sailing craft imaginable; some no bigger than a bidet! These wee vessels float with dignity alongside French yachts, as different as the countries they hail from.

I often cross to swim in the afternoons, on la plage d'Hendaye, a beach that seems perpetually filled with the cadence of French voices. Lying on the hot sand, eyes closed, I imagine them at times as many small birds singing. Parasols of every colour and description dot the beach, and striped canvas cabanas can be hired for an afternoon. In the distance, Spain is always over one's shoulder, with the most majestic mountains imaginable, mysterious with mist and cloud. I can see the church

FUENTERRABIA

high above my village, and the enormous stone wall
that surrounds the citadel.

It all feels rather dreamlike; the sun, the sea, the
sky coming down to drown you in blue. As with most
frontiers, the mix of language and custom conspires to
confuse the senses.

I've been lucky beyond belief with the house,
"Segundo piso" (second floor) with air and light and
all village life in the street below. The houses of
fishermen surround me and all that I need is just
outside my door. There, a marble plaque reads "Oroitza,"
and I've discovered it is Basque for "remember." I've
named this house "The House of Memory," and it all
seems fitting for a place I've come back to after so long.

I've a table for painting, and a sliver of blue sky
above the tiled rooftops. Balconies overflow with flowers,
with washing lines, and with the sounds of caged
birds singing.

Marie · Louise
NAVETTE HENDAYE-FUENTERRABIA
1 PASSAGE - 1 PERSONNE
TARIF CONFORME A CEUX EN VIGUEUR
GRAFICAS BIDASOA
5049

ESPAÑA

URGENTE

ADIEU, NEW-YORK!

21 · Juillet · SPAIN — FRANC

All Basque life can be viewed from where I write this, and a certain gentleness pervades the atmosphere. Beneath the plane trees, Basque men sit in berets, speaking and passing the time together. The urgent chatter of women with prams pausing below my window does little to disturb their sleeping babies. All manner of fruit and vegetable spill out of their shops, and there is a vitality of commerce in the air. A stick of bread peeps out of every shopping bag, and the sound of small children laughing floats up to my window while I write this.

You can feel the sea in everything, especially in the rhythm of the day. There seems a quiet dignity in these people, along with a certainty about how to live life.

Dear Tenn, it has all conspired to make me feel well, and _muy, muy_ _contenta_.

I'm thinking of you across the Atlantico...

Mille tendresses,

B.

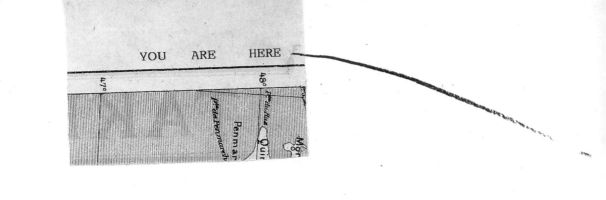

YOU   ARE   HERE

By land

By air

By sea

F R A N C E

28 ·   JULY

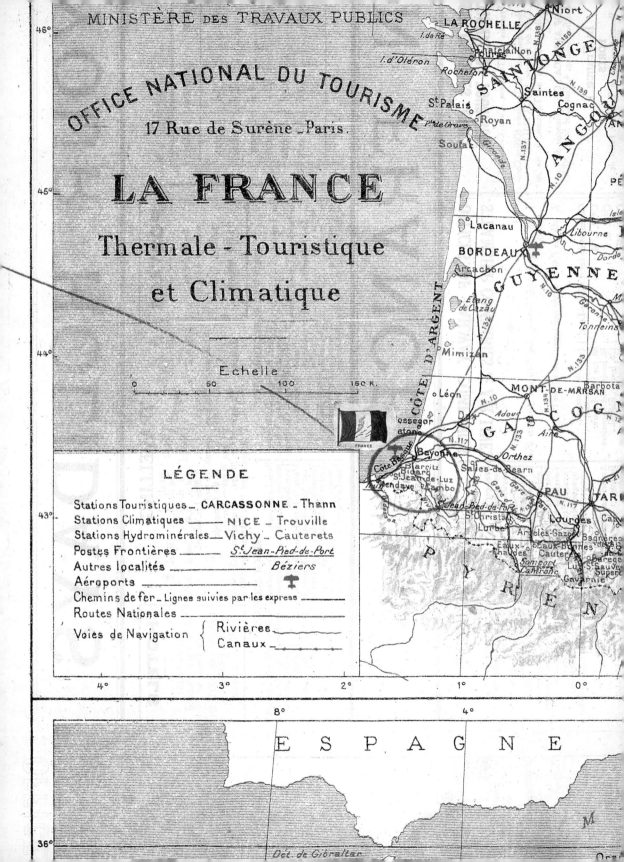

MINISTÈRE DES TRAVAUX PUBLICS

OFFICE NATIONAL DU TOURISME
17 Rue de Surène - Paris

LA FRANCE

Thermale - Touristique

et Climatique

Echelle

0   50   100   150 K.

LÉGENDE

Stations Touristiques	CARCASSONNE - Thann
Stations Climatiques	NICE - Trouville
Stations Hydrominérales	Vichy - Cauterets
Postes Frontières	St Jean-Pied-de-Port
Autres localités	Béziers
Aéroports	✈
Chemins de fer - Lignes suivies par les express	
Routes Nationales	
Voies de Navigation	Rivières / Canaux

ESPAGNE

34 Ships and the Sea Les Bateaux (*m.*) et la Mer

Types of Vessel
steamer le vapeur, le steamer; le paquebot (*with mail and passengers*)
Atlantic liner le transatlantique
cargo vessel le cargo
fishing boat le bateau de pêche
tug le remorqueur
trawler le chalutier
launch la chaloupe
dinghy le youyou
barge, lighter le chaland, la péniche
ferry le bac; le ferry(-boat)
lifeboat le canot de sauvetage
tanker le pétrolier, le navire-citerne
raft le radeau
wreck une épave
hovercraft l'aéroglisseur (*m.*) l'hovercraft (*m.*)
hydrofoil l'hydrofoil (*m.*)
supertanker le pétrolier géant, le supertanker

Parts of Vessel
hull la coque
bows l'avant (*m.*)
stern l'arrière (*m.*)
stern-post un étambot
keel la quille
hatch le panneau; une écoutille (*hatchway*)
hold la cale
propeller une hélice
rudder le gouvernail
deck le pont
helm le barre
gangway la passerelle (de service)
fo'c'sle le gaillard d'avant
alleyway la coursive
rails le bastingage
flag le pavillon
bridge la passerelle (de commandement)
derrick le mât de charge
stabiliser le stabilisateur (de roulis)
engine la machine

boiler la chaudière
plimsoll line la ligne de Plimsoll

Parts of Liner
swimming pool la piscine
dance floor la piste de danse
smoking-room le fumoir
promenade deck le pont-promenade
cabin la cabine
bunk la couchette
port-hole le hublot
deck-chair le transatlantique
covered deck la promenade vitrée, le pont-abri

In Harbour
landing-stage le débarcadère
crane la grue
jetty, pier la jetée
buoy la bouée
lighthouse le phare
home port la port d'attache

Discomforts
sea-sickness le mal de mer
rolling le roulis
pitching le tangage

People
sailor le marin
ship-owner un armateur
chief mate le second
engineer le mécanicien
stoker le chauffeur
radio operator le radio (de bord)
officer of the watch un officier de quart
purser le commissaire
pilot le pilote
stevedore, docker le débardeur, le docker
survivor le survivant
castaway le naufragé
stowaway le (passager) clandestin

Equipment
jersey le chandail, le jersey
life-belt la bouée de sauvetage

" But

watching ocean liners

on the horizon

from her bedroom window

soon produced stirrings

of wanderlust ..."

Bahia de la Concha

San Sebastian

TODAY I'VE DECIDED TO LIVE THE LIFE OF JAQUES-HENRI LARTIGUE. IT WAS THE SUMMER OF 1930, AND HE WAS FALLING IN LOVE WITH RENÉE, HERE IN THE BASQUE COUNTRY. I'VE COME TO THE HOTEL LONDRE PERFECTLY SITUATED ON THE SEA OVERLOOKING LA CONCHA, AND THE MOST ENCHANTING BAY IMAGINABLE. FROM MY BALCONY I CAN SEE THE ISLA DE SANTA CLARA, AND THE LITTLE BOATS OF LOVERS GOING FOR A DAY EXCURSION. IN THE MORNINGS, THE OLD MEN MEET TO PLAY PELOTA, AND TO SWIM IN THE SEA. THE WOMEN OF SAN SEBASTIAN SAY YOU GROW BROWN HERE IN A GOLDEN WAY A HUE RECOGNIZABLE THROUGHOUT THE PROVINCE. YOU CAN FEEL THE PROXIMITY OF FRANCE; IN THE WALK, THE DRESS, AND A CERTAIN SUBTLE CHIC TO EVERYTHING. THEY SAY IT'S THE FRENCH RIVIERA OF SPAIN, AND IT'S EASY TO IMAGINE WHY RENÉE AND LARTIGUE BEGAN THEIR LITTLE STORY HERE.

Julio

Remitente   Domicilio

60 TELEFONO
60 TELEPH

60 BAÑOS
60 BATHS

Renee / Pays Basque 1930

Jacques - Henri Lartigue

60 HABITACIONES
60 ROOMS

SPAIN

SAN SEBASTIAN

Marque LL

It's a San Sebastian sky as I write this; that magical moment
of the day here when the sun sets over la Concha. The ritual of
el paseo is about to begin. I can feel the street come alive;
to walk, to talk, to take the sea air and meet with friends,
this is the time of day for being outside with the family. By
the church Buen Pastor, the sound of children playing fills up
the air. The sweet shop is full of their laughter and movement,
whilst mothers sit talking, taking the last of the sun.

In the Basque Country, the children reign. Pampered and
protected, coddled and cosseted, indulged and adored--not
spoilt--just very well loved.

Prams and pushchairs,hair ribbons and petticoats,
little coloured ballet slippers on strong brown summer legs.
In restaurants and bars and public places, the children are
always welcome here. The street is their kingdom, you can feel
their vitality. A child is a reason for pure happiness here.

It's that magical hour of the day, the time that I love, when
the children reign.

Un momento dulce...

Mysterious, majestic mountains, lush as an Irish
landscape and rained on just as often. I wind my
way down the coastal road, through switchbacks and
industrial towns nestled in steep valleys; one face of
Pays Basque, its split personality. From fertile farms
to fierce factories, how it changes from one moment to
another.

Finally, the first glimpse of the sea. It is staggering,
all delicate blue-green distance—a pristine open sky.
From Zarauz, you can make out _el raton_, a spit of
land off Getaria shaped perfectly like a mouse,
crouched at the edge of the water. Behind it, like
cardboard cutouts, the mountains lie in layer after
layer. The road from Zarauz is dreamlike; sheer rock
dropping straight down to sea. The road hugs the coast
while pine-scented forests press down off the   while
pine-scented forests press down off the

mountainside. One can be completely alone here; just
sea and sky and little benches of repose, so perfectly
placed. I glide down off the mountain, downshifting,
then up again, glimpses of blue between the pines.
For a moment, the Basque Country is mine alone; just
the sound of the surf and the smell of the sea. It's
as if I'm in an emerald embrace.

(Taking the coast road...from San Sebastian to Deba)

The road to Zarauz

is dreamlike.

Bilbao

They call her "the nautical widow..."

It's true she's like an old madame: A bit down
at heel, a hole in her stockings at times. Ah,
but such dignity. She's been robbed of many
things, but dignity is not one of them. No one
could take that away.

A river flows through her heart. Great ships have
passed through her soul. In the "Seven Streets"
one feels her wisdom, and some forgotten, faded
elegance. She may be the nautical widow, but
she's become young at heart again...a new
romance has made her bloom. You can feel all of
this as you walk her streets, breathe her air,
smell the sea in the distance.

They call her the nautical widow.
A river flows through her heart.
Great ships have passed through her soul.

· AGOSTO · MADRID · 38° CENTIGRADOS·
¡QUE CALOR!

I'VE COME BY OVERNIGHT TRAIN THROUGH THE MOUNTA
ACROSS THE PLATEAU OF CENTRAL SPAIN. IT'S LIKE A
WILD-WEST LANDSCAPE, DRAMATIC AND DRY... A
DIFFERENT FLAVOUR ALTOGETHER FROM THE GREEN HILLS
OF PAYS BASQUE. MADRID BAKES IN A SUMMER
SUN, LAZY AND EMPTY — LOOKING FOR ITS SHADOW.
I GO TO THE LORCA EXHIBITION, FULL OF HIS
MEMORY. LETTERS (CARTAS), PAINTINGS (PINTURAS)
POEMS (POEMAS), FRIENDS (LOS AMIGOS), AND
FAMILY (LA FAMILIA). IT FILLS YOU UP WITH
SPAIN — JUST LOOKING. THERE'S NUEVA YORK
IN 1928, WITH COCKTAILS + JAZZ AND LORCA LOOKING HAPPY. I THINK OF
YOU IN MANHATTAN, AND ME — IN MADRID
ON A DAY OF MUCH MEMORY...
LORCA'S AND MINE.

Recuerdo

192?

Foto · L. Buñuel · 1925

AGOSTO · MADRID · MARTES

VOCABULARY
(VOCABULARIO)

LOS AMIGOS (FRIENDS)

MUY IMPORTANTE

LAS CARTAS (LETTERS)

NUEVA YORK (HOME)

POÉTICO

TRANQUILO

THE WAY
I FEEL
TODAY IN
ESPAÑA

LORCA Y BUÑEL EN 192

TO EAT IS

TO LIVE . . . .

· BASQUE PROVERB ·

The Three

Most Frequently

Asked Questions

in

Pays Basque:

"What did you have for
lunch yesterday?"

"What are you having for
lunch today?"

"What are you thinking
of having for lunch
tomorrow?"

Manzana, Merluza, Melón
Patata, Pimiento, Plátano
Calamares, Carne, Cava
Pescado, Panecillo, Pollo

FABRICA DE CHOCOLATES

PEDRO MAYO

CHOCOLATE FAMILIAR A LA TAZA

How I love to order food
here...the words seem
delicious as they roll
off my tongue.

No detail is too small.
No time taken too long.

"To live is to eat."

LA COMIDA

THE CAFÉ CON LECHE OF THE MORNING HOURS.

THE PINTXOS DISPLAYED IN EVERY BAR BY NOON.

THE "ESPECIALES" AND MENU DEL DIA.

I CAN TELL THE HOUR OF THE DAY BY
THE SOUNDS IN THE STREET BELOW; THE SERIOUS
BUSINESS OF SHOPPING HAS ITS OWN SPECIFIC SONG.
WOMEN WITH BASKETS AND CARTS GO FROM ONE
SHOP TO ANOTHER, CONFERRING ABOUT THE
FRESHNESS, THE SIZE, THE SHAPE, AND THE COLOUR.
QUEUES FORM AT THE BUTCHERS AND BAKERS. THE
SERIOUS BUSINESS OF COMMERCE HAS BEGUN.

OFTEN WHEN I AM PAINTING I FEEL THE FRENZY
OF THEIR LAST-MINUTE DETAILS OF SHOPPING; A
GREAT BABBLE BORDERING ON PANDEMONIUM. AND
THEN, CUED BY SOME SILENT, SACRED SIGNAL,
EVERYTHING GOES DEAD QUIET.

NO TRAFFIC, NO SOUND, NO MOVEMENT IN
THE STREET BELOW. ALL IS REPLACED BY THE
GENTLE MURMUR OF FAMILIES AT THEIR TABLES:
A CLATTER OF PLATES, A MOTHER SHOUTING
"VEN AQUI" ("COME HERE") TO HER CHILDREN,
A FISHERMAN CLIMBING THE STAIRS, HANGING HIS
BERET, HOME FOR LUNCH. THERE IS
COMFORT IN THIS TIME OF DAY. ORDER IS
RESTORED. SILENT STREETS, GOOD FOOD,
CONVERSATION, A REST FOR THE BODY AND SPIRIT.

"TO LIVE WELL IS TO EAT WELL"—
AND THE SMELLS FROM ALL THE KITCHENS
SURROUNDING ME DRIFT UP THROUGH MY WINDOW
WHILE I WRITE THIS. AFTER LUNCH I'LL HAVE MY
SIESTA, MY SILENT TIME IN A SPANISH AFTERNOON.

Miramar

Today the sea is high.
There is a great quietness in everything. It has stolen
the beach in the night, along with the
flotsam and jetsam of yesterday's storm.

There is an aura of stillness, everything azul.
A lone gull cries overhead, and after it follows the sound
of nothing.
Today the sea is high.
There is great quietness in everything.

10 Agosto, España / El día de San Lorenzo

Dear Tenn,

I'm leaving for inland France tomorrow, an excursion I've been looking forward to since my arrival. So much has happened since last I wrote. Life seems like a film playing out before me.

Here there seems time for everything, and the rhythm of the day takes you in. A time to walk, to talk, to take a coffee, to meet with friends at the end of a day. It creates a peaceful place inside of you and

what was the

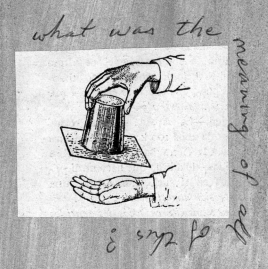

meaning of all this?

I see why the expression tranquila is used so often here.

On the other hand there is an incredible affection for noise, music, dancing, shouting and general mayhem! I have to tell you of the fiestas, the desfiles, or parades, that pass by my window more often than not. It's like a dream really, some mornings I hear them coming before I am awake, and I go to the huge French windows, taller than me, to see what will be in the street below.

My first day here was amazing. I heard the music initially. One hundred or more Basque boys in red berets, carrying huge oars, came first in line. They were followed by two long rows of fishermen, silent and sombre in their stride. In the midst of this came a beautiful woman dressed in a fabulous frock, obviously the queen of all this festivity, carrying a huge box atop her head. Bringing up the rear were enormous papier mâché figures, as tall as my balcony: a fisherman, his wife, a woman carrying a set of keys, and various grotesque figures that chased the children in the street, hitting them with what looked like balloons! You could hear their shrieks of laughter over the flutes and accordions of the band, a frenzy flashing by my window.

All of this passed by as if it were the most natural thing in the world. After, the village resumed its normal pace, while I continued to fantasize over my breakfast. What was the meaning of all this? It seems there is something like this passing by my balcony two or three times a week. I'm beginning to grow accustomed to it it's a part of life here. On Sundays, four men come playing drums and flute in the early morning hours. They start at the top of the village and make their way through all the streets. I've discovered it's a Sunday ritual, a town cry of sorts, to wake the village on this sacred day. I was completely mystified the first time it happened, but it was lovely to go back to bed and hear them disappear deep into the village. I could just barely make out the last notes of the flute while I drifted back to sleep.

The children have so many fiestas to look forward to here. One ends and another begins. From the grandmother to the youngest child, absolutely everyone joins the life of the street for these impromptu parties and parades. No one is excluded, not even I, la Americana. To be Basque is to know your place in the world. And I'm reminded of my initial affection for a people and place I came to know many years ago.

I've been adopted by the upstairs neighbour, Magdalena. I've grown accustomed to my doorbell ringing and finding another little present laid out on the stairs. She speak in an extremely loud voice when she thinks I don't understand (which is often the case), but the more I say "No entiendo," the louder she becomes.

I've learned to smile and say "claro," even when I haven't a clue, and we've become the best of friends. I know for her I must seem rara, a woman far from home in a small Basque village.

I see from my window that the sun has just come out, and Frantzia is waiting. I'll take the ferry across the bay, then drive to St. Jean de Luz, and Biarritz by noon. I hope to swim and then carry on to Sare, a charming village on top of a mountain. I'll take lunch there under the plane trees, where an old friend will join me.

Oh Tenn, how much you would enjoy the peacefulness of this place. I'm sending many kisses, as always, and muchos abrazos.

B.

tickets and timetables
menus and maps
cambios and currency
   par avion and passports
      the endless ephemera of movement
         and of leaving home

"You don't really long for another country,
you long for something in yourself
that you don't have or haven't
      been able to find."

Villages :

Biarritz

St. Jean de Luz

St. Pee

Bayonne

am a traveller but you remain

Fuenterribia

San Sebastian

Bermeo

Perdenales

Bilbao

Crossing the border

the green hills open out

and you can feel France in everything.

Sheep graze on the hillside, oblivious to sheer cliffs dropping to blue sea below. Enormous towers of rock rise up from the water. Waves break across the horizon line. Today the sky is aquamarine; it's the first time I have really understood that colour. The sea is the colour of the sky as I drive on through Frantzia, a touch of autumn in the air. Tall stand of pines to my right, Atlantico to my left. A lone ship passes on the horizon.

Today the tourists are gone. I've a feeling of the season being over. Now the locals will reclaim their villages, their beaches, their shops. There's a sense of space again, of peace and empty roads.

(Côte Basque, Frantzia)

COTE BASQUE,

All day going from village to village, looking for a room.

It's the time of holidays, something we had not

anticipated. "Je suis desolée" each proprietress says,

before telling us they have no room. It sounds so

dramatic. Bidart, Biarritz, Bayonne . Pilar's

persistence is what finally secures us a room. St. Jean

de Luz, beside the sea. We are all pleased.

We go to Sandales Bayonne to buy espadrilles, in

celebration. I choose Basque Blue, to match the colour

of the sea and the sky. I slip off my New York shoes

and on go the canvas slippers with rope bottoms.

We shake hands all around.

Everyone is happy.

SKY

WHERE DID YOU GET

THAT

BLUE?

BIARRITZ

AOUT / AUGUST. CÔTE. BASQUE.

Rounding the coast road to Biarritz, it's true she's like some royal queen, majestically perched on the Bay of Biscay, with her palace and little caprichos below. It was here that great fortunes, fashion, and families in exile came. With her shell-shaped cove and chambre d'amour: all follies of a forgotten time. Hortensias on the hillside. The love light-house, and the Villa Eugenie. I can close my eyes and perfectly imagine her here, presiding over her Court, on this promontory, this perfect bay beside the sea. The miniature gardens with their dollhouse feel, the little benches upon which to rest.

To watch the sunset over Biarritz is to experience a sort of feminine enchantment. Waves break onto the little stone bridge built out over the sea, to the tiny island-sheer fantasy.

It is best to come here in winter, when the town is empty, and its magic can be discovered in a hidden passageway or two. You can have her all to yourself-even the sunset is yours. You can hear the rustle of her skirt when the tides come in...Biarritz, the royal queen.

2297

BIARRITZ

I'VE TAKEN A ROOM IN SARE. AFTER LUNCH WITH MY FRIEND, I FELT COMPELLED TO STAY. THE BALMY AIR, THE VINO TINTO, THE DAPPLED LIGHT OF THE PLANE TREES LINING THE SQUARE; IT ALL CONSPIRED TO KEEP ME HERE, IN THIS VILLAGE I KNEW SO LONG AGO.

LAST NIGHT THE STARS CAME OUT SO CLOSE, ATOP THIS MOUNTAIN. SILENCE, AND A BIG FULL MOON THAT ROSE UP SLOWLY. I SUPPOSE IT'S THE SAME MOON THAT LOOKS DOWN ON YOU.

AND NOW THIS MORNING I OPEN THE SHUTTERS TO A DELICATE BLUE SKY. A ROOSTER CROWS ACROSS THE VALLEY. A LONE DOG BARKS. I CAN SEE ALL OF VILLAGE LIFE BELOW ME. BOYS PLAYING PELOTA, A FARMER STOOPED IN THE SUN PLANTING HIS HUERTO. NOT A CLOUD IN THE SKY WHILE I WRITE THIS. A ROW OF PLANE TREES, WITH THEIR PECULIAR, MELANCHOLY SHAPE. AN OLD CASERIO, THE TRADITIONAL FARMHOUSE OF THE BASQUE, ON TOP OF A HILLSIDE, CATCHING THE SUN. THE MURMUR OF FRENCH VOICES FLOATING UP TO ME.

HERE MY FRIEND'S GRANDFATHER CAME IN THE SPANISH
CIVIL WAR, WHEN HE AND HIS FAMILY HAD TO FLEE. HE
PASSED MANY YEARS HERE IN THIS QUIET VILLAGE, WHERE
ON A CLEAR DAY HE COULD SEE SPAIN IN THE DISTANCE...
THE PLACE HE LOVED, AND WAS UNABLE TO RETURN TO.

THERE'S A CERTAIN WISTFULNESS TO SOME PLACES, AS IF
THEIR MEMORY CLINGS TO THEM. A LITTLE SADNESS HERE,
SO CLOSE IN THE SHADOW OF SPAIN.

I open the shutters to a delicate blue sky.

"TO PIERRE AXULAR, THE BASQUE WRITER WITH THE MOST BEAUTIFUL USE OF LANGUAGE, I, LOUIS LUCIEN BONAPARTE, LOVER OF THINGS BASQUE, HAVE DEDICATED THIS MEMORIAL."

"THERE IS NO REAL HAPPINESS NOR IS THERE A DAY WITHOUT CLOUDS EXCEPT IN HEAVEN."

"À PIERRE AXULAR, L'ÉCRIVAIN BASQUE
AUX PARLER LE PLUS BEAU,
MOI, LOUIS LUCIEN BONAPARTE, BASCOPHILE,
J'AI DEDIÉ CECI."

"IL N'Y A DE BONHEUR NI DE
JOUR SANS NUAGE QUE DANS LES CIEUX."

"ES DAGO ATSEDENIK TA ODEI GABE EGUNIK
ZERUETAN BAIZIK."

FOUND TODAY INSIDE THE CHURCH
AT SARE.

for the special monetary unit composed of various European currencies in fixed proportions, used as a standard against which to assess the value of any particular currency, or as a currency in its own right.

bas mitzvah. See **bath mitzvah.**

basnet. See **basinet.**

Basque *bäsk, n.* a member of a people inhabiting the western Pyrenees, in Spain and France: their agglutinative language: (without *cap.*) a short-skirted jacket, or a continuation of a bodice a little below the waist.—*adj.* **Basque** of the Basques or their language or country. [Fr.]

bas-relief *bas'-ri-lēf*, or (It.) **basso-rilievo** *bäs'sō-rēl-yā'vō*, popularly **-relievo** *bas'ō-ri-lē'vō, n.* sculpture in which the figures do not stand far out from the ground on which they are formed. [Fr. and It. See **base²**, and **relief.**]

bass¹ *bäs, n.* the low or grave part in music: a bass singer—often in Italian form **basso** (*bäs'sō*), *pl.* **bas'sos, bas'si** (-*şi*): a bass instrument, esp. (*coll.*) a double-bass.—*adj.* (of a musical instrument or voice) low in pitch and compass.—**bass'-bar** a strip of wood on the belly of a violin, etc., under the bass foot of the bridge, to distribute the vibrations; **bass clef** the F clef on the fourth line of the stave; **bass drum** the large

---

ash: to attack heavy blow: thing that, w hat (*slang*); ueer-bashing, ng malicious rs of) groups ave a try: to ing), on the rob. Scand.] modest: shy, —*n.* **bash'ful**‐ e abash.]

kish irregular ad.]

guage using a ebra. [Acro‐ olic *I*nstruction

ctification from abstricted:— **Basidiomycetes** of fungi, charac‐ including the

THE WAY

BASQUE PEOPLE

SEE

THEMSELVES ...

D EAR ARAN

THIS CHAP STANDS GUARD ACROSS THE STREET,

SWELTERING UNDER A SPANISH SUN.   ONE WANTS TO

SHOUT

URGENTE

A GLASS OF WATER PLEASE !

I'VE BEEN THINKING OF OUR

FIRST TIME HERE, AND

HOW MUCH

WE LAUGHED . . .

AFTER

GRAN BRETAÑA

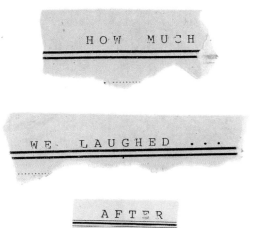

I'M SENDING THIS

EXPRES

WITH MUCHOS BESOS

The

four most

important words

in the Basque

language:

AZUCAR BLANQUILLA • Peso Neto 10 g.
R.S.I. N.° 23.519/VA

Ama		Mother
Aita		Father
Amona		Grandmother
Aitona		Grandfather

AZUCAR BLANQUILLA • Peso Neto 10 g.
R.S.I. N.º 23.519/VA

FIESTAS.

FUENTERRABIA

SEPT.

DEAR HARRY,

   I'VE NOT SLEPT FOR DAYS...

IT'S FIESTAS. 4,000 BASQUE MEN
HAVE MARCHED PAST MY WINDOW
PLAYING
"TXIRULAS (FLUTES) AND ATABALS (DRUMS)
WHEN I DO FINALLY SLEEP, THE
TUNE SO APTLY NAMED
         "TITTI-BILITTI"
              DANCES IN ME
                 HEAD!

CALLE SAN PEDRO
(MY STREET)

FROM MY
BALCONY "LOS
GIGANTES AND
   CABEZUDOS"
(THE GIANTS AND
THE BIG HEADS)
PASS BY LIKE

HUGE APPARITIONS
CHASING
CHILDREN

THE VIEW FROM MY WINDOW

THROUGH THE STREETS
SPONTANEOUS PARADES OF TEENAGERS
ERUPT AT NIGHT— SINGING AND
DANCING AND BEATING ON POTS
AND PANS AND BOTTLES
BENEATH MY WINDOW.
I'M EXPECTED TO THROW
A BUCKET OF WATER
ON THEIR HEADS—
IMAGINE! THEY SIMPLY
SHRIEK WITH DELIGHT.
IT IS ALL
RATHER MAD
AND WONDERFUL

ONE OF
"LOS GIGANTES"

LOVE,
B.

"There are no borders or frontiers with music.

It reconciles us to ourselves

and each other."

SEPTIEMBRE

The fiestas are finished. I sleep now with silent streets. I've been thinking about music. Next to conversation, a Basque likes to sing and make music more than anything. Despite having longed for these silent nights to return, I realise I am missing their music, those spontaneous bursts of song floating up through my window at night making me smile.

EN LA NOCHE

Words of weather...

Tormenta

storm

Tempestad

Tormentoso *stormy*

Viento *wind*

Lluvia *rain*

Esta lloviendo *it is raining*

Nube *cloud*

Nublado *cloudy*

Galerna *wind storm from off the sea, found in the north of Spain*

My dear Tenn,

We've been having a heat wave-36 degrees centigrade, almost too hot to move some days. I've taken to having a siesta in the afternoons, just like the locals. One should never mistake repose for laziness…for these siestas have become a necessity.

Ringed in by mountains and facing the sea, one can watch the weather arriving.

Here, the storms sneak in with stealth. The cloud crouches over the mountaintops, and the storm descends with great gusto. I close the big wooden shutters tight, and wait for it to pass. After, the air is soft, like a caress, and the sea goes all calm and quiet again.

Tonight as I write this, the heat wave is finally breaking. Thunder rolls over the mountain tops, in a continuous murmur, and I feel the gods are angry. So great is the noise that I'm unable to sleep. The sky is flashing with lightning. A cool breeze blows through my window, rustling the papers on the desk.

They say that a giant serpent sleeps under the Pyrenees. Tonight I believe it has awakened.

Goodnight dear Tenn. I know tomorrow this will all seem like a dream. Everything will be fresh and renewed when I go out to post this.

Besos mil y sweet seuños,

B.

HERE—
THE WEATHER IS
LIKE AN OLD FRIEND

WHATEVER ITS
MOOD

IT IS ALWAYS

ACCEPTED...

BAROMETER

Vacuum.

TIEMPO

Agosto/Barrio de Pescadores/Fuenterrabia

The sea is the most delicate of blues today. Below
my window it's the black tobacco voices of two
fishermen I hear, speaking about the weather and
the sea; the two are inseparable.

You can feel the sea in everything. Its rhythm is
like an unseen clock. In the evenings, one can watch
from the port the procession of boats returning with
the day's catch. Like a little parade, they glide in
off the sea, and take their places in the bay.
There's a certain majesty in all of this.
I never grow tired of watching.
And always the women are waiting.

From Biarritz to Bilbao, the Bay of Biscay is the
heart of a Basque.

B A R I O   D E
P E S C A D O R E S

From   Biarritz

to Bilbao,   the Bay of

Biscay is the heart

of a

Basque.

ko-or-day-na'-
co-ordinates.
r-dee-nar'] va.

] f. tomar una
k.

    wine-glass,
own (of hat);

va. to corner
ise.

-par-tee'thee-
er, associate.
ro] m. cup-

y] m. aigret,
tail (of pea-
o —, to be
ard; de alto
sons).
    abundance;

va. to copy,
ural, to copy

o'so] adj.
t, ample.

l m. copyist.
ong, ballad;

coquetería [ko-kay-tay-ree'a]
f. flirtation, coquetry.

coracero [ko-ra-thay'ro] m.
cuirassier.

coraje [ko-ra'hay] m. courage,
dash; passion, temper, 'state',
fury.   [coral.

coral [ko-ral'] adj. choral; m.

corambre [ko-ram'bray] f.
(pile of) hides.

coraza [ko-ra'tha] f. cuirass;
armour plate, ship's armour.

corazón [ko-ra-thon']   m.
heart; courage; **con el — en la
mano,** openly, frankly; **no le
cabe el — en el pecho,** he is
very jumpy, he is on tenter-
hooks.   [tie; cravat.

corbata [kor-ba'ta] f. (neck)-

corbeta [kor-bay'ta] f. cor-
vette.   [charger.

corcel [kor-thel'] m. steed,

corcova [kor-ko'va] f. hump.

corcovo [kor-ko'vo] m. leap,
bound, curvet (of horse).

corchete [kor-chay'tay] m.
hook, clasp; hook-and-eye;
bracket; constable, bailiff.

corcho [kor'cho] m. cork, cork-

SAN SEBASTIAN

Today an excursion to San Sebastian, famous for rowing races, _las regatas_. I've been invited by friends to a house perched over the sea, like a beautiful ship about to set sail. You can stand at the window and be _el capitán_ for the day, with only sea and sky out in front of you.

Today—mal _tiempo_—the sea is stormy, the weather tempestuous and turbulent. Dark clouds settle over the water. Blustery and cold, no boats run today. We sit in the house, the house that seems like a boat, talking about the weather, passing the time, watching the bad mood of the storm. Inside we are warm and content.

The word for storm here is _tormenta_. I've always loved that word and today I know why. There are certain times when a language and a place perfectly suit each other and today is one.

I

dreamed I was

sailing

on a

beautiful ship

in

the

Bay of Biscay

I've bought a new bed. It seems this bed has come full of dreams. The first night, they came immediately upon falling asleep—everything soft, as if I were underwater.

I dreamed I was sailing on a beautiful ship in the Bay of Biscay, with Biarritz in the distance. In this dream I could speak Spanish perfectly, and I was telling stories with all the crew sitting at my feet. There was only water, and the feel of wind through my hair, and hot, hot sun on my already brown face.

It is almost evening now, and soon I'll prepare for bed; my new bed, my bed of dreams.

For John

who lived and loved life with me here

and for our son Tennessee

who was born here.

Fecha 23 Noviembre, 1998

"Vivamus atque amemus...

Da mi basia mille

deinde centum..."

Credits and Permissions

All reasonable effort has been made to contact the creators of text excerpts and/or artworks used in this book; any omission is unintentional and notice of such should be sent to the publisher for inclusion in future editions. The author would like to express her appreciation to the following for their kind permission in the use of materials in this book: Cover, pages 1, 3: Photograph by Michael Judge, used with kind permission of the photographer; Page 5: Quote by Antonio Machado, "Proverbios y Cantares," from his book Campos de Castilla; Page 8: Quote from a book by G. Maugras quoting Mme. Du Deffand (1697-1780); Pages 11, 14: Attribution of quote unknown; Page 13: Photograph of Lorca courtesy of Fundaciûn Federico Garcia Lorca, Senora Tena, Calle Pinar 23, 28006 Madrid, Spain; Pages 16-17: Quote inspired by the poem "Little Gidding," by T.S. Eliot; Page 23: Map courtesy the French Tourist Board, Paris Office of Tourism, Avenue des Champs-Elysees 127, 75008 Paris, France; Page 25: Page from A French Vocabulary for Advanced Level, by I.C. Thimann, Tho. Nelson & Sons, Ltd., Nelson House, Mayfield Rd., Walton-on-Thames, Surrey KT125PL, England; Page 25: Attribution of quote unknown; Page 29: Photograph by Jacques-Henri Lartique, 1930, courtesy of Association des Amis de Jacques-Henri Lartigue, Mme. Martine d'Astier, 19 Rue Réamur, 75003 Paris, France; Pages 34-35: Photograph © Walter Cotton, used with kind permission of the photographer; Page 39, 41:

Photographs courtesy Fundación Federico Garcia Lorca, Senora Tena, Calle Pinar 23, 28006 Madrid, Spain; Page 46: Artwork courtesy Pedro Mayo Chocolates de Navarra SAL, Polígono el Soto, C/ Feunte Vieja 13, 31195 Aizoain, Spain; Page 47: Artwork courtesy Don Hugo, Josu Orma Aecxi, Restaurante Ikusgarri, Avenida Madariaga 11, 48014 Bilbao, Spain; Pages 48-49: Artwork courtesy Panaderia Garmendia, Calle Santiago 59, 20280 Fuenterrabia, Spain; Pages 50-51: Photograph by Fred Hill, used with kind permission of the photographer; Page 56: Quote by John Cheever, from The Stories of John Cheever (New York: Knopf, 1978); Page 57: Photographer unknown; Page 63: Photograph lent by kind permission of Arantxa Azurmendi; Page 67: Photograph courtesy of Andre Leconte, 38 Rue Sainte Croix de la Bretonnerie, Paris, France; Page 76-77: Parts of image taken from Imagenes Inolvidables de Guipozcoa, El Mundo del Pais Vasco, Carreteda Bilbao No. 2048004, Bilbao, Spain (Carlos Garcia tel. 944 739100; Juan Carlo, Pasqual, facsimile 944 73 91 42); Pages 83-84: Artwork courtesy of Cafes Aitona SC, Poligono Bidebitarte, Paseo Donosti 26, 20115 Astigarraga, Spain; Page 86: Attribution of quote unknown; Page 95: Photograph used by kind permission of the estate of Patxo Icaza de la Sota; Page 99: Photograph courtesy of the archives of Emilio Castillo, Juan Maria Bello, Club de Remo de Hondarribia, Molla Ibelbidea, 20280 Fuenterrabia, Spain.

Except where indicated above,
all photography and artwork is by Beth Nelson.
Edited by Marisa Bulzone. Graphic Production by Deirdre Duggan.
Book and cover design by Beth Nelson and Melanie Random.

To

STEWART, TABORI, CHANG
115 WEST 18TH STREET
NEW YORK CITY

NEW YORK
10011 U.S.A.

VÍA AÉREA
PAR AVION

20P

FRAGILE

AIR MAIL

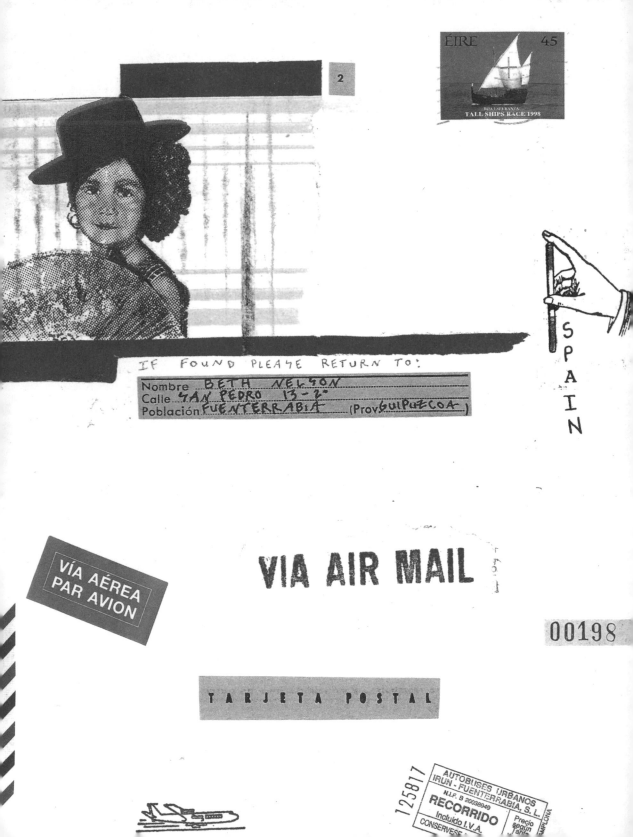

ÉIRE 45
TALL SHIPS RACE 1998

2

S
P
A
I
N

IF FOUND PLEASE RETURN TO:
Nombre BETH NELSON
Calle SAN PEDRO 13-2°
Población FUENTERRABIA (Prov. GUIPUZCOA)

VÍA AÉREA
PAR AVION

VIA AIR MAIL

00198

TARJETA POSTAL

125817

AUTOBUSES URBANOS
IRUN - FUENTERRABIA, S. L.
N.I.F. B 20038949
RECORRIDO
Incluido I.V.A.
CONSERVESE
Precio
según
Tarifa